From Inmate To Boss

By: E. Fresh

ISBN-13:978-1973977889
ISBN-10:1973977885

Cover Design: Crystell Publications
Book Productions: Crystell Publications

Printed in the USA

From Inmate To Boss

DEDICATION

I dedicate this book to my wonderful mother, Leah Harris, who always stuck by my side, and my two brothers, Malik and Marcus.

CONTENTS

E. Fresh

Chapter 1
The Right Attitude

The Right Attitude Towards Success

It is extremely important that you have the right mental attitude towards success. You have to picture yourself as a success already. In order to achieve it, you have to first believe it. The right attitude also includes positive self-talk—telling yourself that you're great at whatever it is that you plan to achieve. You have to have the "can do" attitude towards your goals and whatever you're trying to accomplish. "Impossible" has to be blocked out of your vocabulary. You have to wake up thinking about success. It has to be a burning part deep down in you that solely focuses on your success. What foods are you feeding your subconscious? You have to be hungry for success. What positive thoughts are you meditating on? Are you watching and reading positive motivating material? Be careful of who and what you take in. If you take in slum, then you will give out slum.

Fresh Point: I kept my attitude positive. I read all positive books. I went to sleep thinking about success and woke up thinking about success. I knew that I wanted to start my own company so I was motivated to be my own boss. I knew that if I could image something, then it wasn't farfetched or out of my reach. I researched my topic well and had a notebook of material of the things I needed to do to accomplish my goals. I sorted the people out who had done what it was that I wanted to accomplish. Believe me, most people don't mind sharing some insight to those who show themselves worthy of such information. When I first started writing, I asked successful authors that I knew many questions about writing and different techniques about being published. I now have acquired my own writing style and share some of my own learned techniques in this book.

PUT YOUR GOALS IN WRITING
SET DEADLINES

Putting your goals in writing helps you to see your goals clearly and is a reminder of what you want to achieve. Setting deadlines helps you to strive towards completing the goals that you have set. The first part to accomplishing a goal is to think about what you plan to do. The second and important part is to write it out. Writing your goal out is like a mission statement. You can actually see what it is that you intend to accomplish. When you write your goal out, you should place it somewhere where you can constantly see it or be reminded of your goals. Don't write it down on a piece of paper and tuck it away. This defeats the purpose of writing it down in the first place. Writing your goals down and hanging them on the wall is a good reminder because you will see them a few times a day. It is also a good idea to have a notebook that you write in and go through daily. If you get into a habit of writing your goals and to-do list together, it will be hard for anyone to knock you off track.

Setting deadlines helps you to stay focused and not to get completely off balance. Give yourself reasonable time frames when setting deadlines. Don't try to accomplish a goal or task in a time frame that is close to impossible. For instance, if you're trying to write a book for the first time, it would be unwise to give yourself thirty days to complete the book. This would be an almost impossible task for a first-time writer. Now, if you have already been through the process, then it may be a little easier to accomplish. For even the more seasoned writer, a month is by far pushing it. You should be flexible with your deadlines. If you don't make your deadline by the time you intended, it's not the end of the world. Just extend your current deadline and give yourself a little more time. The bright side is that you're still closer to completing your goal than you are to beginning your goal. No one can say that they always make their mark on their deadlines every time. You have to take into account certain situations that are out of your control. Say if you get sick for a few days, this will take you out of the flow of things. Now you're a few days behind because of something you had no control over. Extending your deadline by a week or two will put you back on track. This is why being flexible makes completing your goals easier to bring to fruition.

Fresh Point: I write all my goals down and hang them on my wall. I'm constantly reminded of the different projects that I must complete. I can honestly say that I can never say I have nothing to do. However, I can say that sometimes I'd rather not work on some of the projects that I must complete. Writing my goals down on paper and hanging them up helps me to maintain focus. Seeing is believing! After I think of my goals, I write them out to get a clearer, more vivid picture of them and so I don't forget them. Once I start working on a goal or project, I always set a deadline to when I plan on having completed my task. Sometimes I deliver on my intended deadlines.

Other times I'm definitely flexible with my deadlines. My deadlines are not written in stone. The times that I must extend my deadline, I'm normally at least halfway close to completing my task. Sometimes I may need to just take a day off so I don't burn out. There have been times when I'm ready to write and I have everything ready to begin, and I can't get a word out. Then it's times when I'm working and don't want to stop. At those times I have to force myself to stop so I can get a few hours of sleep. With setting deadlines, I learned to respect the process; some days will be better than other days. But as long as you continue to aim to the completion of your goals, you'll make out fine. Setting deadlines gives me the important aspect of striving to complete my goals.

A LITTLE EVERY DAY

There is no need to rush or to put too much on yourself by racing to complete your goals. If you do a little a day, it will all add up. A little quality each day is better than a lot of quantity. In other words, if you put every effort into producing or providing substance, it will be worth more and appreciated much more than to just be providing or producing mediocrity efforts. Just as having a balance, it's good not to overload yourself and burn yourself out. Make striving towards your gifts or practicing your talents seem natural. Every day won't be fun, but every day doesn't have to be or seem overwhelming. For an example, most of us put our pants on one leg at a time. You wouldn't just try to jump into both pant legs at the same time. The main point is that you don't have to put unneeded stress on yourself by forcing more out of yourself than you have to give.

A little every day gives your body, mind, and spirit time to get off to a fresh start and flow at a better pace. A little every day also helps you focus better. You may even see things that you may have not caught. Some days you may feel tempted to do a little more than usual. There's nothing wrong with having a surge of energy and wanting to stay in the creative flow of things. Even employees do overtime now and then. But I haven't heard of a job where employees are allowed to do overtime every day. The reason for this is that local rules and policies mandate work conditions. The same reasons apply for working on your gifts or talents. Only difference is that there is no one waving a policy over your head when it comes to working on your gifts or talents on your own spare time. But you're still at risk from the same effects from burning out, crashing, being overwhelmed from working too hard. You're in charge of yourself, so it's extremely important how you manage your complete self. Don't become one of those people who hate what they do because it leaves them no time for anything else.

Fresh Point: I learned firsthand what it means to be overwhelmed. I even went to sleep early and woke up in the morning earlier to get more done. At the end of those days I was exhausted, completely worn down. I was trying to accomplish too much throughout my day. For example, I would be working on two different writing projects at a time. I would try to at least write a chapter at a time on both projects throughout the day. I would be forcing myself to write even if I didn't feel like it. This kind of pressure only overwhelmed me and wore me out. I took a step back and then started a little every day. Now I work on one project at a time. If I'm writing, instead of me forcing myself to write a complete chapter at a time, I allow myself the freedom to finish a few pages at a time. If I feel like writing more, then I continue to write. But I'm not under any pressure to get done a certain amount or number of pages each day. I found out that this allows my writing to flow more easily. And I'm not regretting the time frame when it's time for me to sit down and write. I actually look forward to sitting down and completing my day's work, working towards my goals. A little every day can be applied to whatever it is that you do.

PROTECT YOUR VISIONS

You have to keep your visions guarded and protect them at all costs. Be extra careful who you share your visions with. Not everyone will be able to see your visions as clearly as you. You will even have vision thieves—people who will try to kill your dreams and visions.

These people are known as dream thieves because they simply just want to ruin your chances of success or happiness because they have nothing better to do, or mainly because they're afraid of your success.

Vision thieves and dream thieves come in many different forms. It doesn't always have to be from your known haters. They can be the people who are in your immediate circle. These people can dress up as your friends, but really be your foes.

This is how you spot a vision or dream thief. Say you always share your thoughts and ideas with one particular person, and that person is always putting your ideas down. This person is a vision thief, and it may be a good idea to stop bouncing your ideas off this person. Another form of vision thieves are the people who are always quick to tell you how your idea won't work or how silly your idea sounds.

You need people around you who are supportive, even if they can't see your vision. Your inner circle should build you up, not be so quick to tear you down. But keep in mind not everyone will get your vision. That's why the vision came to you and not them.

Fresh Point: Early on I had people try to steer me off my goals. People would say to me, "How are you going to put your book out? What makes you think you are going to be successful?" Many people said discouraging things to me about me being focused on my goals and tasks at hand.

I had to learn how not to reveal certain things around certain people. I learned to let my finished products speak for me. As time would have it, the same vision thieves now ask for advice from me about writing books and starting a business. Even those people who hate on you with negative energy will eventually come around. Those who are smart will understand that you have already traveled down the same road that they're trying to embark on. Who else better could help them avoid the bumps and stumbles along the way? In all things the dark always seeks towards the light.

HAVE A SUPPORT GROUP

Having a support group consists of a few trusted people whose opinions you value who will give you honest feedback. Your support group can consist of relatives, friends, associates, convicts, inmates, whoever…as long as the people you choose are not yes-men people, not people who will tell you just what you want to hear. You should also be able to be of some assistance to those in your support group. Maybe you give them honest feedback on the things that they take part in. Or you help them out by lending a helping hand when needed. Perhaps you're a shoulder for them to lean on. An extra set of ears for them when they need to just be heard. However it goes, you have to give and take. You have to give a little to be able to take a little.

Your support group doesn't have to be a large group. Wherever you're at, you can find support for your legitimate effort close by. Whatever your passion is, there's a similar group that will fit your chosen field. For example, if you're into art, then check out an art class. Not only will you find support, you may also be given the opportunity to use a wide range of equipment that you otherwise had out of your reach. If you're into acting, then join some sort of drama program. Not only will you find support from the drama department, you'll be able to hone your acting skills by practicing and performing for the drama department. Your support group will enable you to bounce ideas off of each other. You have an inside crowd who you will be able to test your material on first, thus giving you a proof of concept, sharpening your professionalism.

Note you shouldn't just invite anyone into your support group. If the person has no interest in the things which you are involved in, then you should not have them in your support circle. What kind of support, advice, input can you honestly expect to get from someone who doesn't share your interests?

Fresh Point: It is extremely important to have a support system. I found a common ground with other writers that I know. I even took advantage of my surroundings and found the new commits who are always looking to read something because of their boredom. These new commits be more excited to read anything that they can get their hands on, since they have nothing to read. Given that it's always a handful of new commits, I get to test my latest projects and get a few different responses. Seeing and hearing their responses helps me test my proof of concept.

As I stated earlier, I also have a few other people who write in my support group. No matter the subject, writers always have plenty of material that can use an extra set of eyes or ears on. So having like-minded individuals in your support group is always a plus. Your support group should motivate you and encourage you to continue to work towards your set goals and be willing to assist you in accomplishing your goals. Of course you should be willing to assist and perform all the same tasks for the members in your support group that you ask of them.

SUCCESSFUL PLANNING

At the end of each of the following chapters I have included two goal worksheets that will help you see your goals more clearly. The worksheets help you take your thoughts and turn them into planned ideas, then turn your planned ideas into goals, while providing you with a time schedule that you set, allowing you to complete your goals. The Goal Sheet allows you to write down your short-term goals. The Goal Action Sheet allows you to write down your long-term goals. Both worksheets provide you with a timetable to be able to keep referring to, allowing you to stay on target and measure your progress.

I actually use both of these two sheets today. When I'm starting a new project, I use the Goal Sheet, which I refer to numerous times before I complete the project. It is a needed blueprint for myself that helps keep me focused. The Goal Action Sheet I use all the time. I keep blank sheets with just the questions on it. The reason is I'm always adding to the sheet. Once I complete a goal, then I set new ones for myself. I'm always trying to raise the bar for myself. If I don't achieve what it is that I planned to accomplish, then who can I blame besides myself? The Goal Sheet and the Goal Action Sheet allow me to see my goals clearly and work towards them. Both worksheets are extremely helpful and should be constantly referred to.

GOAL SHEET

What goals do you want to set for yourself?

_____

_____

What time frame do you plan on achieving these goals?

_____

_____

How many hours a day are you willing to sacrifice in order to accomplish your goals?

_____

_____

Who are the people that you may go to for help in accomplishing your goals?

_____

_____

GOAL ACTION SHEET

Where do you see yourself one year from today, and what are you doing to help prepare yourself?

_____

_____

Where do you see yourself five years from today, and what are you doing to help prepare yourself?

_____

_____

Where do you see yourself in the next ten years, and what are you doing to make sure you accomplish these goals?

_____

_____

How bad is your desire to accomplish these goals, and are you prepared to follow through with the goals that you have set?

_____

_____

CHAPTER 2
SOUP AND WATER

SOUP AND WATER

To reach your goals, you have to have the "soup and water" mindset. You will be required to invest your hard time and energy. You owe it to yourself to set aside time to focus on your goals. Time is the most precious resource that once it's gone, you cannot get it back. So every moment wasted is time that you will never get back. No one will want you to succeed more than yourself. Everything that you need to succeed, you have it at your fingertips.

When it's time to get down to business, you can't be partying and just having a good old time. If you have to invest some funds to complete your goals, you can't be eating lobster and shrimps on the regular. You have to budget to get things done that are important to your goals. Think about your successful future before you ball out with a new pair of sneakers that you really don't need. Are you going to worry about your image or your future? Do you have to spend every dollar that you get? What wants can you go without?

Fresh Point: Soup and water really meant soup and water to me. Instead of me going to commissary and getting a bunch of junk, I really cut down and bought the bare minimum. I would only buy a survival kit that consisted of mainly soups. When I was hungry, I would eat a ramen noodle or two and drink some water. I wasn't eating for the taste, I was just trying to fill me up. I was on a budget and I had a bigger focus. I had to accomplish my goal of putting this project out. Success takes sacrifices. I even cut my cable off. I had no time to pay to watch other people on television getting paid. If it didn't come on digital television, then it wasn't for me. I was consistently thinking about advertising, promoting, and seeing myself on television. I gave up a lot to chase my dream. Me not chasing my dream would have cost me a price that I wasn't willing to pay. My success was worth it to me. One way or another, we all will have to give up something temporary to gain more in the long term. I'd rather eat like a king every day instead of just for one day.

WHAT'S YOUR PURPOSE?

Each of us was born with a purpose and born to live out our purpose. Knowing this is the easy part. The hard part is determining what's your purpose? Your purpose may even come to you easily. It's possible for your purpose to be facing you soon as you wake up in the morning. Others may see your gift or talent in you and may even be able to spot and develop your purpose. You may need to be coached or have a mentor help guide you. You may have to seek out the thing or things which you were called to do. For example, I know this guy, they call him Jigaboo Jackson. Whenever Jigaboo Jackson is near, people know not to make eye contact with him. Jigaboo Jackson will talk you to death. If he's walking by himself, he'll sing loud to himself. If a person looks sad, he'll even try to cheer them up by doing a happy dance for them. Jigaboo Jackson even takes pride when working for free. He does the jobs that everyone else refuses. Now to everyone else, Jigaboo Jackson is annoying and a buckeye. To me, I see his outlook and his purpose. Jigaboo Jackson is a great people person. Whatever job, whether minor or major, he's going to do his best, singing a happy tune. This is the kind of person that you'll want to serve you at any restaurant or answer your questions at any company. We all know a Jigaboo Jackson.

Now back to discovering your purpose. Spending time—days, hours—will help you discover your natural purpose. Once you find what you're meant to do, do it to the best of your abilities. If you diligently seek out your purpose, you will be rewarded and find your purpose.

Fresh Point: My purpose is to motivate others, either by writing helpful information to motivate them or by speaking to motivate a crowd of people, as long as I get to motivate others by any vehicle that I may reach others. My purpose found me in high school in Language Arts class while writing an assignment. My teacher submitted a journal writing of mine to a magazine company without my knowledge. Imagine my surprise when my teacher informed me that my writing was accepted and she needed my signature for my consent. Since that very moment she has encouraged me to continue to write. Before I even thought about writing and being published, this wonderful lady believed in me and saw something in me first. I will forever be grateful that she coached me along. So as I said earlier, some people may spot your purpose in you first. It's just up to you to develop your purpose and step into it.

INVEST IN YOURSELF

Investing in yourself is taking the time out to find out what you love and what gets you motivated. Once you find out what things it is on this beautiful earth that you enjoy doing, you have to cultivate the things which you enjoy. At first it may not just come to you; you will have to try different activities to see what you enjoy doing or what activities come to you naturally. It may not be something so easy that you find out right off the bat. It even may take some time for you to listen to yourself and try numerous activities.

Just as with sports, no professional athletes become good at their chosen sports the first time around. The great spend many hours practicing to become great. Investing in themselves sometimes meant sacrificing other things for the sport which they wanted to become great at. It takes time to develop the skill set of a professional. But when most professional athletes are interviewed and asked the question whether or not they would trade the dedication and sacrifices it took for them to get where they are now, I haven't heard one athlete say that the time they invested in themselves was not worth it to get to where there are at now in their lives. The same thing goes for taking the time out to find out the things in this world that you enjoy and may love doing. Again you have to give yourself the chance to learn. Try practicing new things, investing in yourself and seeking the knowledge about a chosen activity that you have always been wanting to acquire. If you won't take the time out to invest in yourself, how can you expect someone else to invest in you, whether it be someone else listening to you, someone giving you advice, someone mentoring you, or someone else helping you out in any kind of way. No one else can be at fault if you don't cherish yourself and take the time out to invest in yourself first.

Fresh Point: I learned that people get more involved in the things that you're the most passionate about. Others can feel the vibe and can become energized off of your energy. I notice that when I'm talking to people about my ideas, they become enthused about my projects. I learned that the first person that I must sell on any idea is myself. Once I speak about or attack my plans boldly, others are interested. But before me speaking of my plans or attacking a goal that I set, I first have to invest the time and energy into putting in the work. I have to believe in myself first. Now when I'm speaking to others about an upcoming project, others are sold the first time around. All this is because people know from past experiences that I will deliver on my goals. Me delivering or accomplishing my goal sets could not be possible without me even taking the time out to invest in myself.

WHO'S IN YOUR INNER CIRCLE?

Who have you invited into your inner circle? Do the people in your circle help you to strive forward? Do they push you and help you bring out the best person you can possibly be? Does your inner circle listen well and care about what moves you? Do your goals for yourself line up with the people in your circle? These are some questions that you should consider when evaluating the people in your circle. If the answer to most of these questions is no, then it's a great idea to tighten up your circle and replace your circle with better company.

You should strive to surround yourself with goal-orientated company. Choose your circle of friends based on the qualities that you like about them. If you want to paint, hang out with the artists. If you are a fitness buff, join a gym and hang out around the pull-up bars. If you're a writer, become a member of writers' magazines or join a writers' group. You will attract like-minded individuals. As the saying goes: "Birds of a feather flock together." If you're constantly spending your time surrounded by negative individuals who don't want much out of life— people who are just wasting their lives, a bunch of hip dummies—then you can expect the same results out of life that those hip dummies have. Not everyone will be proud of the fact that you're trying to accomplish something out of life and do better for yourself. You won't have all cheerleaders cheering you on. Without a doubt you will have to leave some people behind, even family. If you admire the people's lives who you are surrounded by on a regular basis, then by all means, your circle is tight. But if you want better for yourself, then you must change your thinking, your entire outlook, and especially your inner circle if they're not about changing for the better.

Surround yourself with those people who have accomplished in life what you're trying to accomplish. Find a mentor from someone who is already successful in the field that you want to master. There are multiple organizations that sponsor mentorship programs. If you're unable to find a mentor, then turn to other resources. The Internet has information on every topic. If you're not computer-literate, then there are numerous books written on every subject.

Fresh Point: My inner circle consists of a small group of individuals. I take my time seriously so I'm cautious about whom I let in my circle. I have no time for hip dummies.

When I started to embark on the road to change, not everyone was happy with my decision. I had to disconnect with childhood friends. I broadened my horizons. I made allies and associated with different individuals who I would have never even talked to. I stepped out of my comfort zone and reached higher. I surrounded myself with the people who accomplished the things in life that I wanted to accomplish. For example, before I even was published, I would seek out others who I found out were published. I would get to know them and ask them different questions, just picking their brains. I would even treat these individuals to an ice cream, a pack of tobacco, something to compensate for their time. This made them more willing to talk to me. In reality I made out because I was able to gain knowledge from others who have walked the path that I was traveling. I learned by experience that if you show thyself worthy, people will help point you in the right direction.

APPRECIATE YOUR RESOURCES

Your resources are the people in your life who support you, whether they give you mental, physical, or financial support. Your resources are those people who make achieving your goals less difficult. It's the people who make a difference in your life, whether they be your legs, handling the things such as making your calls, assisting you in your everyday business activities, handling things that would otherwise be difficult for you to accomplish without them. They could be the ones who will loan you money when you need them to. They can even be the ones who listen to you when you need to get a load off your shoulders. These are the people without whom your personal / business affairs wouldn't operate as smoothly. The people who give you the best advice—without them you may not stay on top of your game. Your resources could be your family members, friends, pets, etc., whoever makes your affairs easier.

You should show your appreciation to the resources that you have. Since they play such a vital role in your life, you should show them how much you appreciate them. You don't have to do anything extraordinary; it's the thought that counts. Something as simple as buying them a thank-you card, sending flowers to their jobs, remembering the days that are important to them, such as birthdays, anniversaries, celebrations, Mother's Day, Father's Day, etc. Your resources already support you out of the goodness of their hearts. By showing them that you appreciate them and don't take them for granted, they will be willing to continually stand by you and support you in your business endeavors now and in the future. A little thoughtfulness goes a long way. Showing your appreciation to your resources allows them to feel appreciated and makes them feel special, all while giving you longevity.

Fresh Point: My resources / support team make me accomplishing my goals much easier. I remind myself all the time how blessed I am to have the support from them. I try to reciprocate my gratefulness towards them. I have all their birthdays written down so I know not to forget those dates. I write and store all the important events that mean something to them. I know how much Mother's Day means to the women who support me. So I make sure the women know that they're appreciated from me on that day. On

Father's Day I make sure the males know that I appreciate them. For those who have no children, not married, I still let them know that I appreciate them. Again a little appreciation is good for the soul and goes a long way.

LET GO OF DEAD WEIGHT

Dead weight, as referred to in this topic, relates to those people who tie you down, people who cannot add any value to your life. We all know them and have been surrounded by them. I'm speaking of those individuals who always want a free ride. Those individuals who can never pull their own weight or bring anything to the table. The kind of individuals who are looking for a freebie. These are the people who only come around when the times are good. The ones who come around when the sky is blue. The individuals who want to share the glory from your hard work and tears.

These dead-weight individuals I'm speaking about are the ones who you can never count on. The ones who are always missing in action, but somehow come around for the finale. These are the individuals everyone else warns you about hanging around with. The ones who don't have your best interests and are up to no good. Dead-weight individuals don't discriminate on gender. It can be a no-good girlfriend who's unappreciative, ungrateful, and undeserving of your attention. Or it can be a male who doesn't respect and appreciate your friendship. Dead-weight individuals come in many shapes and forms. If an individual doesn't sincerely care about you as a person, if they constantly try to put your ideas down, then watch out and make plans to block these individuals out of your inner circle.

Fresh Point: I have a low tolerance for dead-weight individuals. I learned that these individuals can camouflage themselves in many different ways and wear different coats. I also learned that these dead-weight individuals will suck up all your positive energy. Their whole purpose is to kill and destroy—to try to kill your dreams and destroy your goals. They don't hate like your regular haters. They're more like inside moles. Their job is to get close to you and cause confusion. By all means guard your visions, your ideas, your goals, your gifts / talents from dead-weight individuals.

GOAL SHEET

What goals do you want to set for yourself?

_____

_____

What time frame do you plan on achieving these goals?

_____

_____

How many hours a day are you willing to sacrifice in order to accomplish your goals?

_____

_____

Who are the people that you may go to for help in accomplishing your goals?

_____

_____

GOAL ACTION SHEET

Where do you see yourself one year from today, and what are you doing to help prepare yourself?

_____

_____

Where do you see yourself five years from today, and what are you doing to help prepare yourself?

_____

_____

Where do you see yourself in the next ten years, and what are you doing to make sure you accomplish these goals?

_____

_____

How bad is your desire to accomplish these goals, and are you prepared to follow through with the goals that you have set?

_____

_____

CHAPTER 3
MOTIVATE THYSELF

MOTIVATE THYSELF

When it comes to motivation, you must dig deep inside yourself. Whatever ritual that you may have to do to get you motivated, whatever music, self-talking to yourself, drinking coffee, etc., that you engage in to get you focused, this is the routine that you must perform to get your brain activated to perform your main objectives. You cannot depend on someone else's drive to push you or depend on their creative flow to get you started. I'll repeat it again: You cannot depend on someone else's drive to push you or their creative flow to get you started. Each individual is responsible for his or her own creative progress.

Some people need a few cups of coffee before they can start their creative thought process. Others may need to hear certain types of music to perform their duties. Some may even engage in positive self-talk to ease them into the creative or work flow of things. I've even seen people who have a compulsive cleaning habit that before they work, they have to clean up, or else they will not get off to a good start. If you have to walk or run a mile before you tackle your goals, then lace up your running shoes, start your engine, and prepare for the journey ahead.

I know of people who listen to certain motivational speeches or read inspirational quotes before tackling their goals on a daily basis. Maybe it is a certain shirt or piece of clothing that inspires you to perform to your maximum potential. You might be motivated by thinking about a special someone, past or present, in your life and reflecting back on some encouraging words that person and you shared together. If you focus your efforts on doing your best and completing your positive goals, then you could envision a better future, a brighter tomorrow. Just by thinking of one's known goals and plans for the future, whether it be tomorrow, in a few months, or even a few years, may be just enough to get you aiming high and shooting for the stars.

Fresh Point: I learned that I have to be my very own light when it's time for me to be motivated, writing from a place where it is always dark and gloomy. By dark I mean surrounded by negativity. A good percentage of those people who I pass by daily are still lost or trapped and confined in the same world that got them in their current situation. They're not sick and tired of coming back and forth to prison. So looking for inspiration from these individuals would be setting oneself up for failure. By gloomy I mean it's a good percent of individuals who lost hope. They are the ones who express less desire for anything to come out of life. So with myself I overly motivate myself. I think about my end game plan. I picture myself already at the top of my game. I think about the sold-out stadiums of people who will pay and come out to hear me speak and motivate them. I think about the positive difference that I'll be able to make in the lives of others. Remember, each individual is responsible for his or her own goals. It is up to us to think, plan, and work towards our dreams, goals, and better future. It's up to us to become the best self that we can be. Nobody else is responsible for our own progression in life but our true self.

KNOW YOUR VALUE

Knowing your value is extremely important. The things that matter the most seem to be the most important aspects in our lives. Your mind, time, and energy should be amongst the most precious resources of yourself. So putting an important value on yourself is by no means too much. If anything, by not assigning an important value to yourself, you leave open the door for other people to devalue you and whatever you bring to the table. Your time, mind, and energy are by far the most important resources that you have to offer this world and others. Taking yourself seriously is a statement of what's in your mind, body, and soul that shows on the outside of you that you're serious about yourself and the many things which you engage in. Great minds spend days, months, years discovering the great ideas of the past and future ones to come. "Great minds discuss ideas; average minds discuss events; small minds discuss people." Quote by: Eleanor Roosevelt.

Others will see you by how you present yourself. So if you present yourself as average, then you will be seen as average. If you present yourself as being great and striving towards greatness, then others will be forced to recognize your greatness. Just look at the best musicians in music. In order for others to consider them amongst the best or the greatest in the business, the musicians first had to make the great music that stood the test of time. I'm sure the musicians who are listed amongst the great didn't go into the studio and make average music. They knew their value even when others didn't, and they made believers out of everyone else who didn't believe in their talent.

Value yourself and your time even if others don't. Eventually those who don't believe in you will believe in you or get left behind. Either way, never devalue yourself and what you have to offer to this world. See yourself now as the best in your chosen field. This positive self-thinking breeds confidence in yourself. This positive self-thinking helps you work towards your own greatness. Don't just settle for being good or average—work towards being great. Master your talent, gift, or craft. Identify your strengths and what you're able to bring that makes you unique. Add your own signature, your own flavor, your own style to what you have to offer. Bless the world with what you have to offer, but don't settle for less of anything that's underappreciated of you. When you know your value, you learn your worth. See yourself at the finish line of completing your biggest goals and imagine the feeling. After soaking up this feeling, work towards this and don't allow anyone to block your path.

Fresh Point: I learned to value myself, my time, mind, and energy. No one else will value you more than yourself. My mindset with me comparing my value is that I'm wealthy with the resources that I'm blessed with. So I never allow another to devalue my talent, gift, or my time. I believe in myself even when others may doubt. For example, when I wrote my first book, I was offered a contract that I believed was far less than what I believed my efforts were worth. Other authors who I consulted with told me that the deal was average for new authors. Well, me believing in myself and knowing I could make more money than I was offered, I didn't sign the contract. I published the book myself, kept my rights, made my money back, and had numerous people write me asking what else is to come. I knew my value and had the confidence to continue walking on my journey, even though I may have had some slight delays along the way. Understanding my value has allowed me to stay focused and walk boldly.

POVERTY OF THE MIND

Your mind allows you to achieve whatever it is you can imagine. If you lose your ambition, your spark, and stop brainstorming and dreaming of new ways to be successful, then your mind won't paint these images for you. Instead, your present will be your future. Your mind will still give you images, but they may not be the images that are best for you. You'll get stuck with the "why try this?" attitude, the handicapped mindset. You have to feed your mind the positive thoughts that you want to achieve. Once you train yourself to think these positive thoughts, your mind will expand with powerful thoughts beyond your control. You will constantly envision great ideas in your mind. Any ideas that you conjure up in your mind can be your reality. You will have to continue to put in the work necessary to achieve your thoughts and goals.

The mind is our greatest asset. It allows us to see what our individual self can accomplish if we work towards it. Napoleon Hill understood this philosophy greatly. Half of his life he studied how one acquires the things which they most desire. His research from interviewing countless successful people was that there is no limit to what one who truly desires can accomplish. Napoleon Hill found the same trait in all the successful people he interviewed.

The common trait was that all the people first had envisioned themselves as being successful with the ideas they thought of. They then attacked their thoughts and goals with everything that they had. They also all had plenty of setbacks. All were determined to be successful and let no one block their path. Each of the successful people that Napoleon Hill interviewed had, sometime in their lives, people who doubted them and didn't believe in their vision. Had these people listened to those doubters, they wouldn't have made it to the mega successful status they acquired. These people were able to get rid of the poverty mindset by attacking their goals and living their dreams.

Fresh Point: I trained my mind to think positive thoughts. Once I got used to feeding my brain successful thoughts, my brain just ran off. Sometimes the thoughts and visions that I get, I can't begin to see how I conjured up the ideas. But knowing the end result is extremely motivational. I remember when I was about nine years old, my grandmother asked me what I wanted to be when I grew up. I responded, "Grandmom, I want to be rich." My grandmother told me, "You're rich with love now." Now my mind is rich and I'm rich in thoughts.

HAVE A BALANCE

Whatever gifts or talents that you have to offer to the world, you must have some sort of balance. Every hour and minute of the day cannot be spent on just developing your special talents. You can't go all day focusing on you and your desires. If you do, you will quickly get overwhelmed, even burned out, to the point where you may even have a nervous breakdown, possibly be hospitalized. You may even need to seek professional help. This is why you must have a balance. It can be something as simple as taking some time out of your day and talking with the Creator.

You may need to enjoy having a good breakfast or spending time talking to your loved ones. You may feel good if you're visiting the sick or poor. You may have a ritual of visiting a religious place daily to pray. Or you may feel good by going to the gym daily. You may even enjoy helping the elderly or having power talks or long conversations with them. You may even enjoy exercising daily, this may get your wheels turning. You may even find that you like to work on your gifts or talents while you're at work. Or you may find yourself more relaxed when you're at the library. You may even like to take long walks daily. Some people have special television programs that they must watch daily or their day is thrown off. Some people even have daily planners they write in so they can know what to do and be reminded of what times frames are allowed for each activity. There is no right or wrong way to go about balancing your day. Whatever is legitimate that keeps you moving forward, striving towards your goals, is your balance. Balance is needed so you don't burn yourself out and so you have different things to look forward to. So when you get working on your gifts or talents, you have fresh eyes and a fresh perspective to perform at your best.

Fresh Point: My balance consists of numerous things throughout my day. First I try to wake up positive by thanking God Almighty for allowing me to see another day. I then get myself together, then I eat breakfast. Throughout the day I try to speak with the people closest to me. Seeing them or hearing their voices makes a huge difference and can be a boost of energy for me. I make sure throughout the day that I have done some type of work that is edifying to me, whether it be me reading, researching for a topic that I may need to know more about for a project that I'm working on; whether I do some writing for an upcoming project that I'm working on or plan to work on; whether I take the time out to contact different businesses to see how they may be of some assistance to me and my business, inquiring what different forms of services they offer that will help my business grow.

GOAL SHEET

What goals do you want to set for yourself?

_____

_____

What time frame do you plan on achieving these goals?

_____

_____

How many hours a day are you willing to sacrifice in order to accomplish your goals?

_____

_____

Who are the people that you may go to for help in accomplishing your goals?

_____

_____

GOAL ACTION SHEET

Where do you see yourself one year from today, and what are you doing to help prepare yourself?

_____

_____

Where do you see yourself five years from today, and what are you doing to help prepare yourself?

_____

_____

Where do you see yourself in the next ten years, and what are you doing to make sure you accomplish these goals?

_____

_____

How bad is your desire to accomplish these goals, and are you prepared to follow through with the goals that you have set?

_____

_____

CHAPTER 4
THE ENTREPRENEUR
SPIRIT

THE ENTREPRENEUR SPIRIT

Being an entrepreneur gives you the freedom of being your own boss. There is nothing like getting paid for doing the things which you love. There is an old saying that goes, "If you enjoy doing what you love, then you'll never work a day in your life." Everyone has some sort of God-given talent or gift. The most common reason for people committing crimes is for financial gains.

If you look at the whole criminal web, you will see that there are plenty of roads that lead to criminal acts, but the main road is for financial gains. But given the energy that goes into negative thinking that leads to criminal acts, if that same energy is channeled into focusing on harnessing one's positive ideas and goals, then instead of prison cells being filled up, the economy would be constantly thriving. There are over a million people in prisons all across the U.S. So as you can see, there is no stopping inmates from being entrepreneurs. Former or currently incarcerated, the numbers stand on entrepreneurship.

Whatever your talent or gift is, if you're good at it, people will pay for it. This is where you turn your talent or gift from a hobby to a business. If you are an artist, then people will pay for your creative artwork. If you're an artist and are incarcerated, then your first customer base should be your fellow inmates. Not only do you have a good test audience, you have a legitimate way of making money.

If you're an aspiring musician, play writer, or actor and incarcerated, then you can harness your talents by being involved in whatever plays, talent shows, church performances, etc. that your institution offers. Don't overlook the chapels. They're the first place to welcome performers and will let inmates practice and rehearse when it's not affecting their services. Again, your fellow inmates will be a great harnessing tool who will indeed keep you sharp. Whatever your talent is, there is a way to sharpen your skill set. Whether it be a class to further educate yourself or an outlet for you to strengthen your skill set, your fellow inmates will help you get to the next level.

Fresh Point: While I was working on writing this book, I looked for any similar books that were on the market. I found plenty of motivational books, but none directly towards inmates (former or current) on the topic of becoming entrepreneurs. So with me writing this book, I recorded my whole process from beginning to end. I tested my concept by actually doing everything that's written in this book.

When I completed the first rough draft, I tested my

concept by allowing a few good men to read a couple chapters. Their responses all in awe, eager to read more, just proved my concept that this book was needed. Since I'm a writer, I signed up for a writing class that was offered by a college. I even volunteered to be an assistant director for a play that the chapel conducted. This helped me to see how a live crowd responded to my writing. This taught me how to write in writing groups, a skill that will continually come in handy and pay off. As you can see, not only have I harnessed my writing from my in-house audience, I also write inspirational, motivational content to help my audience reach their next level.

DON'T BE AFRAID TO FAIL

Failing is a part of life's hard, tough lessons. Failing only hurts the most when you stay down. But everyone who experienced failure and overcame has been taught a good lesson that comes along with it. Failing also gives you the experience needed for the next time around. Failing makes you appreciate some things a little more. It makes the victory that much sweeter. Failing gives you the lesson of getting back up and trying again. Failing teaches you the lesson of resilience, enduring through the good and the bad. Failing teaches humbleness and meekness. Failing teaches dedication to those who overcome, and teaches lessons about avoiding the same or different pitfalls in the near future. Failing teaches those who overcome how to be grateful and appreciative. Failing teaches those who overcome the importance of a helping hand—and the importance of helping a worthy person going through what you had experienced and overcame.

If you never experienced hurt and cried, then you wouldn't appreciate laughter and happiness. Every failure teaches a lesson on how to master the task better. Failure is considered a loss when you give up and quit and accept the failure.

Fresh Point: In life, before you master anything new, you get it wrong a few times first. I remember when I was writing my first book and trying to get it out. It seemed like it took me forever because I didn't understand the writing process. Every time I thought I was moving forward, it became a step back. When I was dealing with a company to help me edit and prepare my manuscript into book form, the company went out of business—not before me paying them and sending them my work. This seemed like a complete failure to me. I had saved my funds and was almost ready to print when I was suddenly left with nothing to show for it.

Talk about a setback. I was hurt and wanted badly to give up. I had to start back over and save from scratch. During this time I reached out to other reliable companies. I networked around to different authors, and I sued the company that burned me. So I learned a valuable lesson that I paid for. I continued on my journey. I got my investment back, and I shared my story with other hopeful authors. When the road looks rough, just keep putting one foot in front of the other foot.

POWER BRUNCHES
MEETINGS OF THE MINDS

Power brunches / meetings of the minds is when you and your support group or like-minded individuals meet up to eat and converse about business, future plans, or projects. The meetings don't have to be expensive. Invite your selected members to a sandwich and a refreshing beverage. Or it can be as simple as a cup of coffee and a candy bar. The main focus is to welcome like-minded individuals to toss around ideas and get feedback from respected peers. Offering something to eat is an incentive to the members who are participating. And for the person hosting the power brunch, this is a frugal way of getting feedback and getting other people excited and involved in your projects. Companies and big corporations have these types of gatherings all the time.

Think about when a new movie is coming out that Hollywood has beat us over the head with promotions. The movie production house gives out a selected number of free screenings with complimentary lunches. Now you can learn a lesson from these companies when it comes to being frugal. When you show up to these company-sponsored events, you may get a four-ounce cup of tea or coffee with two cookies. But you have to respect these companies because they accomplish their end goal by getting you to their event and asking all who attend to fill out a survey.

This is no different from you hosting your own power

brunch. Only difference is that not only do you get feedback (your survey), but along with it giving others the opportunity to get feedback and sharpen up their goals. Now those individuals who take part in your power brunch get a complimentary snack and the opportunity to refine their own goals. Power brunches / meetings of the minds is a win for the host and the participants.

Fresh Point: I normally host a power brunch / meeting of the minds at least once a month. The power brunch consists of about six highly motivated individuals who all have something positive going on. I supply the group with a four-ounce hot cup of coffee or tea and either a candy bar or honey bun. I normally host the power brunches on the last Sunday of the month. It never fails—someone always checks with me to make sure that we are having the power brunch every month. Looking at it from the participants' view, they get a free hot beverage along with a snack and get to polish up their projects. Then looking at it from the host's (my) point of view, the investment is worth the while. I get to test my proof of concept and polish my projects constantly.

PROOF OF CONCEPT

In order to provide a service or have a product to offer to potential customers, you must first see if your products or services are worth it to potential buyers. You may enjoy and even love what you're doing, but if no one is paying you or willing to pay you for your services or products, then the thing that you're doing is just a hobby. When testing out your concept or services, you can start by having a "power brunch" where you would get valued information pertaining to what you have to offer. You can also do research and engage others by asking them for a minute of their time to engage them in a survey, asking them particular specific questions involved with your services, such as asking them questions like if your product or service was made available to them, would they purchase it. You should offer your product or services at a discount to the people who take part in your surveys. After all, they are helping you. Make them feel appreciated. If your product is made for sale, you can offer potential customers your product at a discount, in the hopes of having them as repeat customers.

You can even donate some of your products to a worthy cause. Or donate some of your time to provide your services to a worthy cause, such as to people in need, schools, shelters, hospitals, etc. You can also contact your local news stations when doing these types of charity, providing to worthy causes. This in turns helps spread the positive word about your services. It generates great publicity that you can take advantage of. You have to get out there and rub shoulders with your potential customers.

How is anyone supposed to know that you have a service or product to offer the public? Testing your concept gives you valuable feedback. You learn what your potential customer likes, dislikes, wants, and needs. Cable television networks have been testing their services since the beginning. They allow you to watch a station that they're offering for free for a limited time frame. This is the cable network's way of engaging their audience—giving away free services by offering a limited time frame to watch the station in hopes that the customers will sign up and pay for that new service.

Fresh Point: I use many different ways to test my proof of concept. One way is by having "power brunches." When I'm writing a book, I'll allow a select number of people to read a chapter and I'll pay close attention to their responses. If they tell me that they couldn't put it down and are eagerly ready to read more, I know that my audience will be satisfied. If the people who I selected to read my sample chapter give me the "it's cool" nonchalant response, then I know I have to do an overhaul over the material until I get the desired response that I'm looking for.

DON'T NOTHING COME TO A SLEEPER BUT A DREAM

If you're not where you want or plan to be in life, ask yourself the question: What are you sleeping for? Ambitious people are not lazy individuals. In achieving their goals, there were plenty of restless nights. For an example, look at Steve Harvey: writer, comedian, radio personality, television host—just a few of his titles. Look at how many jobs this man has. Look at his success. When do you think he has time to sleep? Now of course he has to sleep in order to stay rejuvenated. But he has even mentioned himself, on his morning radio show, that he's not sleeping more than eight hours a day. He even said that he barely gets eight hours of sleep. With all the jobs Steve Harvey has, it's easy to tell that he works more than he sleeps. So again, if you're unhappy with your current situation in life, then why are you sleeping more and working less? You don't need ten hours a day or to take naps in the daytime. Those extra hours of sleep can go to completing your goals or honing your gifts. One of your goals should be to work now on yourself to be able to take off and sleep whenever you like after you're successful.

Fresh Point: I have many restless nights where I'm up just working. Some nights, as I stated before, I have to put up my materials and force myself to get a few hours of sleep. But I understand that when chasing success, I have no time for twelve-hour night dreams. The goal is to work hard so when I want to sleep or play hard, I will be satisfied with where I am in life to the point that I'm comfortable with my success. At this point in my life, I still have a lot to complete and I'm too busy chasing success. I'm wide awake for success.

NEVER LOSE YOUR GRIT

Grit is the ability to move on in life after being knocked down, no matter what has transpired. We all face a horrible time sometime in our lives. You must not let the events, past or present, that set you back keep you on your back. You must get back up and keep moving, and if you can't walk right away, then crawl. But by all means, never stay down. In life we all take some sort of fall. Some people fall harder than others. But as the saying goes: "It's not about the fall, it's about the get back up." Or as they say in boxing, "Get up, beat the count." Life has a way of flexing its muscles. Just never let life keep you in a headlock. There are all kinds of situations that make some people just want to throw in the towel. Losing someone close has made people not want to continue on the path they were once on. Some may say that the gift or talent that they once loved does not seem to bring them joy or seem fun anymore. Some give up on themselves too easily and quit prematurely. Just because of life's hardships, don't let them force you into giving up or early retirement.

Now it's different when you've been at something a long time and it's time to let it go. Sometimes you have to know when to hold the cards and sometimes you have to know when to fold the cards. But for this topic I'm talking about never just give up on yourself. Have the grit to get back on the horse when life knocks you down. I'm speaking about not being afraid to take a swing at the ball again. I'm sure no baby ever took its first steps without falling down. That was the first lesson many people learned to get back up and try again. The proof can be seen in every human being who walks. The principles intertwine and correlate together. Never lose your grit, your will, your resourceful courage to overcome the most difficult situations that may arise. When life throws you a curve ball, adjust your bat and get ready to hit the ball out of the arena. Never lose your grit and keep your spirit vibrant.

Fresh Point: I know all about life throwing extremely hard blows. I have been dealt some blows that years later I can still feel the pain. It's more than just keeping my head to the sky. I remind myself that those things that were intended for bad can also be used for good. Instead of letting a situation ruin me, I use the motivating factors to push me forward. By all means I know the feeling of hitting the floor. I felt the feeling of being down. I know the feeling of being up also. As the saying goes: "The top is so much better than the bottom." To me that saying rings true. So just like every morning is a new day, when you're down, you have the power to get back up. Grit is extremely important because when all else fails, when everyone leaves, when all your possessions disappear, grit is what will not allow you to count yourself out. Grit is what forces you to cross the finish line when everyone else has dropped out. Grit helped me to reach my audience (you).

THE GET-IT-DONE MINDSET / BUSINESS MINDSET

The get-it-done mindset / business mindset is the same as investing in yourself. You must have the focus to set goals, set deadlines, and get it done. If you're employed, you won't go into work and do nothing all week on company time. You're on the company's clock, you're getting paid to perform your work obligations. The same attitude and principles apply towards completing your goals. You may not be getting paid at the moment for your efforts, but eventually your gifts, talents, or services have the potential to produce multiple streams of revenue. So then don't shortchange yourself when it comes time for completing your set goals. The business mindset is knowing that your gifts, talents, or services will produce in the long term. Don't just think or plan for today. Set your sights high—think, plan, and work towards the future, whether it be a few months or even a few years. Those who fail to plan, plan to fail. Don't be a part of those who plan to fail by not planning. Picture yourself in the future where you dream of being in your professional life. If you're unhappy now about your current situation, then work towards where you would like to be in the future. Start working on your goals: get it done!

There is someplace on the goals that you have set that you can start working on now. Don't use the excuse that "I don't have the money to start at this moment" or "I can't quit my job at this moment, I have no other finances." Who said you have to start at the beginning or at the end? Start on whatever part you can complete now. If you don't have the funds right at this moment to form your company, start researching who your competitors are and what they offer for their prices. Then see how your competitors reach their customer base. If you're into fashion, attend a few fashion shows.

Mingle with the designers. Study what the buyers are buying. You may not be in the game yet, but be in the building. Prepare for your opportunity. It is better to be prepared for an opportunity and not have one than to have an opportunity and not be prepared. When you prepare and set goals, you're using Intelligence. When you put the time in to complete your goals, you're putting in Effort. When you use your Intelligence plus Effort, you're creating your Opportunity, which equals Success (I+E+O=S). Have the courage to set goals and get it done.

Fresh Point*:* I had to acquire the discipline to stay focused from the time I set a goal to the time I completed it. It took me some time but I finally got good at it. Now I have tunnel vision. When I set my goals and my deadlines, I work tirelessly to finish my projects. For example, when I'm working on a writing project, I'm not satisfied until I have completed the project. If I'm working on a book, then I push myself until I get the manuscript into the editor's hands. Now phase two starts with getting the manuscript to the printer. After that is phase three, promoting the book. So through all three phases, I have the get-it-done mindset while focusing on the business side of things.

IF NOT YOU, THEN WHO?

Ask yourself the question: Who else wants you to succeed more in life than you? If you don't put in the necessary work to make your dreams into a reality, then who else will push you? You have to be your own motivating factor. Who wants your dreams more than you? Who's counting on you more than yourself? If you give up or never try, who would be the first person you let down? Without a doubt the first person who you will let down will be yourself. Before you attempt to save anyone else or attempt to help anyone else find their way, you first must remember the golden rule is self-preservation. Again, before you attempt to help or save anyone else, you must save and help yourself. You cannot help anyone if you're helpless. You cannot teach if you haven't been taught. Before you lead others to glory, you first must lead yourself to glory. I'm not saying not to help anyone else out along the way. I'm saying make sure you find your way first before you attempt to give someone else a hand. Once you are successful and made your mark, help someone else make their mark.

Ask yourself the question: Will anyone else help you to succeed before they succeed themselves? I haven't seen any professional sports team give up their chance to win a championship game to help the opposing team finally win one. Your goals and dreams are your property that's waiting for you to claim it. If you don't push yourself to accomplish the things that you most desire, no one else will lose a night of sleep. No one else cares if they don't have a vested interest. If you don't make your goals and dreams a reality, no one else will make it a reality for you. If not you, then your goals and dreams will die at the graveyard, just as so many others have and continue to do so.

If only the graveyard residents who are at their final resting place could tell their story about the lost goals that died with them. Some might say that they lived out their goals and dreams. Many may say that they wish they would have chased their dreams and goals and done things differently. Don't let your clock run out without you finding out your purpose, fulfilling your goals, and living out your dreams. If not you, then who?

Fresh Point: The statement "If not you, then who?" rings true dearly to my heart. I understand that if I don't apply myself and accomplish the things that I have set, then no one will push me to deliver on my goals. The fact of the matter is that the things that are dear to me mean nothing to anyone else. No one cares until they need you. The same ones who will doubt you will eventually ask you for your support. The point is that your desires can become your reality and be accomplished if you put forth the effort.

REINVENT YOURSELF

You can never be afraid to reinvent yourself. Reinventing yourself keeps you fresh and exciting. If you're unhappy with the results that you're currently experiencing, then plan otherwise and reinvent yourself. Charlie Wilson, lead singer from The Gap Band, reinvented himself when he came back as a solo artist. During his long hiatus, a lot of people counted him out. Now that he has made his comeback, many generations have been blessed with his music. The same thing with Tyler Perry, producer, playwright, screenwriter, and actor. Before he became a mega movie star, he wrote stage plays and slept in cars. Tyler Perry said that he saved up his money and produced one of his stage plays, only for it to flop. He then saved up again, made a few changes, added a gospel singer at the opening of the play. He re produced the stage play, and off to the races he has been ever since.

The same thing with Dr. Dre, producer, rapper. When he left the major recording label Death Row, some people thought he was crazy and would never be able to make great music again. After a long hiatus, he reemerged with a new record label, Aftermath, and one of the biggest-selling music artists (Eminem) today. Dr. Dre still to this day bumps out mega hit records he produces. You can see all these mega stars all went through a down time where they were on a hiatus for a while. Each one of the above-mentioned celebrities has reinvented himself and experienced wonderful comebacks.

Fresh Point: When I decided to take writing seriously, I had to humble myself and reinvent myself. I had to refresh up on some writing courses. It was a lot at the time, me attempting to tackle something new. I had to put in the necessary work to be able to make my goals a reality. When I released my first book, I reinvented myself from my old ways to a published author. Don't never be afraid to reinvent yourself and show the world what you're made of. It may even be one of the best decisions you made in your life.

THINK SMALL, GROW SMALL; THINK BIG, GROW BIG

People who think small, grow small. Think big and grow big. Whatever your hopes, goals, and dreams are, think and plan big. There is no limit to the potential that you set for yourself. So don't limit yourself or allow others to limit your growth for you. How bad do you really want to accomplish your goals? Who's in your way and what's stopping you from achieving your desires? In order to think big, you have to rid yourself of all the small-minded people who surround you. Lambs do not hang with lions! Lambs are prey to lions. The same as big thinkers don't think along the same lines as small thinkers. Big thinkers are too busy making their ideas manifest into reality.

When in training, soldiers are taught to depend on and trust their fellow soldiers in combat. Soldiers have a saying that goes, "No man left behind." Clearly the soldiers' mindset is to think big and accomplish the mission. When setting goals and planning your strategy to carry them out, shoot for the stars. Have the "I can" attitude towards completing your goals and accomplishing your desires. Until you have attained the things which your mind desires, constantly picture yourself already having acquiring your desired goal. It's important to know the end result that your goals will allow you to reach. By picturing your end result, you can always refer to it and take bits of inspiration or motivation from time to time.

Fresh Point: I always think big. Through my talks with numerous people, I realized that not only do people dare to dream, they also dare to think big. It's a sad state of affairs when you witness others who are spiritually broke and left with no hope. My dreams and goals belong to me. No one can steal them if I don't allow them to. It costs me nothing to dream big. It does cost me to chase my big dreams. But ask yourself this question: Which price would you rather pay? The price of being forever miserable and too afraid or lazy to go after your dreams? Or the price of chasing your dreams and living your life to the fullest possible extent? Me, myself, I take the latter answer.

SHOOT FOR THE STARS

Whatever your goals are, make sure you aim high. Shoot for the stars. It's your future. Ask yourself the question: Why not you? Why can't you have the better things in life? You owe it to yourself to picture a brighter tomorrow for yourself. No one wakes up and says, "I want to work cleaning toilets the rest of my life." Not trying to bash anyone who cleans toilets for a living. I'm just stating the fact that you are where you are in life because of your attitude towards life. Politicians grow up thinking and preparing for a career in politics. Karate masters and Kung Fu masters spend their entire lives being students and studying the craft. It takes years for the best to become recognized and become great. There is no difference with where you picture yourself in the future. It will take discipline and dedication to get to where you want to be.

Your sweat, blood, and tears will pay off when you're enjoying the fruits of your hard work. Nothing worthwhile comes easy or overnight. You owe it to yourself to aim high and shoot for the stars. Think about the difference and how much richer your life and the lives of your children can be if you aim high and shoot for the starts. Before you can achieve anything, you first must think or dream up the idea. Ideas are what made America great. If you dream it, you can achieve it. No matter how out of reach your goals seem, continue to aim high and shoot for the stars.

Fresh Point: I'm amazed at the goals that I set for myself. I aim high and shoot for the stars on everything that I can imagine. Once I reach my goal, if I'm somewhat off, I'm not too far off. I'll still be able to reach my target once I adjust and re-aim. The amount of necessary preparation that went into preparing for success makes it less difficult to get back on track. Shooting for the stars helps me put my best foot forward. I always remind myself that anything is possible. Those who contributed great things to this world knew to keep their dream alive. Be sure to not let the dream die in you. Aim high, shoot for the stars, and keep the dream alive.

REACH BACK

Once you have finally achieved your goals, or have become great or known with your talents, remember the road that led you to the success you have. Just as once upon a time you needed guidance and help, reach back and help someone else who you see traveling down the path you once traveled. Lend a helping hand. You can guide an up-and-coming person to help them avoid the same setbacks you experienced. You can even give some advice about the lessons that you have learned. You can even mentor one who's deserving of the chance. You must remember that somewhere along the line, someone has helped you out. We all stand on the backs of those who came before us. Plus you never know when you might have to cross the same paths of those who need you now. One day that person who once needed you may be in a position where you may need their assistance. It will suck if you were mean to this individual prior and now they may be the person in charge who can make or break a deal that you worked so hard for. Now just imagine this same individual remembers you being so nice and compassionate when they were early in their career and struggling. The tables could have easily changed. This person may be the one who's in charge of a festival that you may need use of. You can bet if you treated this person good when they were starting out, you may even have the red carpet rolled out for you. It's a saying that goes, "Be careful about the people you step on your way up because the same people you'll pass on your way down." The people who you help out could potentially become a resource of yours. Remember, resources come in many different forms.

Fresh Point: I try to give back as much as I can. If I see someone who wants to write and needs a little guidance about the publishing business, I try to inform them on the knowledge that I have gained over the years. I also try to point them in the right direction and line them up with reputable contacts. I remember some of the hard lessons that I learned and some hard lessons I avoided by having other experienced people walk me through the process. I always remember that no one gets to be successful all on their own.

GOAL SHEET

What goals do you want to set for yourself?

_____

_____

What time frame do you plan on achieving these goals?

_____

_____

How many hours a day are you willing to sacrifice in order to accomplish your goals?

_____

_____

Who are the people that you may go to for help in accomplishing your goals?

_____

_____

GOAL ACTION SHEET

Where do you see yourself one year from today, and what are you doing to help prepare yourself?

_____

_____

Where do you see yourself five years from today, and what are you doing to help prepare yourself?

_____

_____

Where do you see yourself in the next ten years, and what are you doing to make sure you accomplish these goals?

_____

_____

How bad is your desire to accomplish these goals, and are you prepared to follow through with the goals that you have set?

_____

_____